Prayer Team Training Guide

How to demonstrate God's love and power through personal prayer ministry

Second Edition

Glen Hobbs

1. Introduction

The Prayer Team performs a vital function in the life of the Church. It is principally through this team that we minister to the needs of individuals through personal prayer. We are prayer servants, and brokers of the power and presence of the Lord.

Because we are engaging with people with various backgrounds, emotions, maturity and motives, we have to conduct ourselves with the utmost care and wisdom. We have to be above reproach, protecting the dignity of those to whom we minister as well as the reputation of the church. We take pains to do what is right, not only in the eyes of the Lord, but also in the eyes of men (2 Corinthians 8:21).

It is therefore vital that all members of the Prayer Team conform to the protocols and guidelines in this Guide.

2. What we do

The Prayer Team demonstrates the love and compassion of the Father by praying in faith for the felt needs of the recipient, whether it be for encouragement, physical healing, peace, provision or any other need.

- We use the delegated authority from Jesus to overcome the power of the enemy in the lives of those to whom we minister.

- We use the gifts of the Spirit and cooperate with Him in accomplishing His purposes in the lives of those to whom we minister.

- We edify, exhort and comfort.

- We avoid confusion, offense and harm.

- We avoid drawing attention to ourselves. We point to Jesus, and say as Peter did "*Why do you stare at us as if by our own power or godliness we had made this man walk? ... By faith in the name of Jesus, this man whom you see and know was made strong. It is Jesus' name and the faith that comes through him that has completely healed him....*" (Acts 3:12-16).

- We cheerfully submit to the oversight of the leaders.

3. What we don't do

- We do not give rebuke, correction, or direction.

- We do not counsel or provide any in-depth ministry.

- We do not offer any medical or other professional advice.

4. Qualifications for Prayer Team

- Each Prayer Team member must be a committed attendee of this church. Note, however, that from time to time we may invite others to participate, for example at conferences where there are participants from other churches who are known by the leaders present.

- We each profess Jesus Christ as our personal savior, and have accepted and appropriated the work that Jesus did on the cross to forever deal with our past, present and future sins, and have assurance of eternal life with Him.

- We each maintain a vital, personal walk with the Lord. While this is important for all believers, it is especially important for Prayer Team members!

- We have been baptized in the Spirit as evidenced by the functioning of the gifts of the Spirit in our lives and the (increasing) presence of the fruit of the Spirit. We are to be "being filled" with the Spirit – continuously renewed as we live to please Him.

- We believe that all the gifts of the Spirit are for today, and that the Lord will use each of us as we desire to minister to the needs of others in His name.

5. Expectations of the Prayer Team

- We are prayed-up, faith-filled and enthused (*En Theos*--In God).

- We switch out if not ready to minister or are in need ourselves.

- We model a culture of receiving as well as ministering.

- We have a teachable spirit and are willing to receive correction.

- We have genuine compassion for people –"*Jesus...had compassion on them and healed their sick*" (Matthew 14:14, Mark 1:41).

- We desire to grow and evidence progress in our faith. While none of us are yet perfect, we are exhorted by

Jesus to be perfect! (Matthew 5:48).

- We are committed to securing results, not just to praying!

- We passionately pursue the power and presence of the Lord, knowing that He transforms lives--ours and those we pray for.

6. Commitment Required

- We ask for a commitment of one year, after which everyone is automatically released. The hope however is that you recommit for the following year again!

- Attend the team training times and periodic team meetings.

- On weeks that you have been scheduled to serve, join with the other team members before the service to pray for the service, and wait on the Lord for any words of knowledge. Provide these to the leader on duty before the start of the service. Even if you are not scheduled that week, join in on this prayer time if you are free!

- Be available at short notice. There are times when the Holy Spirit moves and the response to an invitation overwhelms the number of team members on duty. As a Prayer Team member, if the on-duty team is overwhelmed, join in and help without waiting to be called to assist.

- You may be asked to step off for a season, or you can request at any time to step off if personal needs dictate.

7. Protocols/guidelines for Ministering

7.1. Pray with eyes open
You are encouraged to pray with eyes open, for several reasons:

- You can observe the results, and adjust your prayer accordingly

- You can see what's happening around, be prepared if they fall, and better communicate with a catcher if present.

- If two or more are praying, there can be better coordination with the one leading.

7.2. Pray short prayers
- Do not pray long, rambling prayers. People who come up for prayer can rarely remember all that is

said at that time. They will remember how they felt, and the results!

- Likewise the Lord does not need our many words (Matthew 6:7), just our faith (Matthew 21:22, Mark 11:24). As someone once said... *"True prayer is measured by weight, - not by length. A single groan before God may have more fullness of prayer in it than a fine oration of great length."*

7.3. Preferably pray in pairs

- We will attempt to schedule teams accordingly, but there may be times when due to number of people requesting prayer, we may have to pray individually.

- Reciprocally, do not overwhelm someone. Two or three at most is appropriate. Where there is more than one person praying, be clear who is leading. There must be one person leading, the others must follow that lead.

7.4. Avoid praying for the opposite gender alone

- If the person is married, have the spouse present if possible.

- Have a Prayer Team member of the same gender as the recipient join or lead the prayer if possible.

- Be visible to and within earshot of others when praying for someone of the opposite gender.

7.5. Avoid praying for young children alone
- If at all possible, have parents/guardians present. If this is not possible, let the parents know that you prayed for their child.

- Be visible to and within earshot of others when praying for younger children.

7.6. Ask permission to touch the individual
- Ask if you may place your hands on the person. Head, hands or shoulders are generally safe places to touch, but don't presume!

- If the person shows any signs of discomfort, do not touch them.

- If a spouse or parent is present, it is a good idea to have them lay hands on the individual.

- If praying for healing, and if appropriate and modest, you can ask the individual to place their hands near the affected area, and lightly touch their hands as you pray.

- Do not push or pull or do anything that would startle

or offend!

7.7. Confidentiality

- You may hear some personal and painful things while serving on the Prayer Team. Do not show surprise, shock or disapproval. Demonstrate empathy and compassion at all times.

- All information shared by the person must be kept confidential. The Prayer Team leader and the pastors are considered part of this sphere of confidentiality. You must inform the team leader or pastor about any situation that has the potential to produce harm, e.g. suicidal tendencies, spousal or child abuse, or any other potentially serious situation.

- If there is evident need for counseling, ask the person if you can share the need with an leader, or recommend they contact the church office if preferred. Do not offer counsel or direction.

7.8. When to escalate

- At every meeting there should be a designated leader or pastor. Know who that is in the event you need to communicate with them.

- Reach out to the leader any time you feel

uncomfortable. You will encounter some strange situations while serving on the Prayer Team. If you don't know how to handle a situation, for whatever reason, ask a leader to join in.

- Demonic manifestation will occur from time to time. If you do not have the experience, confidence or training to deal with demonic activity, call one of the leaders to take over.

7.9. Dress & Hygiene

- Be neatly and modestly dressed. Leave no opportunity for distraction.

- Be fresh and clean before ministering. Use deodorant well before the meeting. Caution: deodorant itself can be very off-putting if recently applied. Strong fragrances (deodorants, perfumes, after shave) can be problematic to some individuals.

- Get into the habit of carrying and using breath mints.

- Bottom line: make sure there is nothing that can cause distraction from the prayer time.

8. Model for Prayer Ministry

8.1. Lead-In

- Ask for the person's name if you do not know them. Use their name often in communicating with them, and during prayer.

- Make sure the person is comfortable. If necessary, provide a chair for the person to sit.

- Have a catcher present if there is a possibility of the person falling (See Section 9--Guidelines for Catching).

- Explain that we will pray more than once if necessary, provided they are comfortable for us to do so.

- Share a short testimony to build faith in the recipient. Share a recent relevant testimony from church, indicate where you have seen this before, provide a scriptural precedent or share a relevant scripture passage.

- If the person is responding to a word of knowledge, call attention to the fact that that is evidence of God's intent to answer.

- Ask the person to let you know if anything is happening when you pray – hot, cold, pain diminishing, increasing, or shifting.

- Explain that only some of the people prayed for feel

anything at the time of prayer.

- Let the person know they don't have to pray, or have to work up faith, or do anything. That's what we are there for. They should simply close their eyes, be at rest, and just receive.

8.2. Acquire the Target

- In this step we determine specifically what to pray for.

- Ask the person if they are willing to share specifics of the need, but do not push.

- Do not let them go into a long drawn-out description. We don't need to know the back-story. It's not important. We just want to know what the target is.

- Pray for discernment. At times the Lord may give you a word of knowledge seemingly unrelated, something else that needs to be prayed for, or a word of wisdom to know how to proceed.

- Note: In practice, these steps are performed simultaneously with Lead-in, e.g. you need to know what you are praying for before you can share a relevant testimony!

8.3. Select the Prayer

- In 'Selecting the Prayer', you are deciding how to engage in prayer for the identified need. How and what you pray is obviously dependent on the specific needs of the individual you are praying for. Some options are:

  > **Ask:** You can ask the Father directly, in the name of Jesus, to answer the prayer. This is of course appropriate for any prayer need, ranging from healing, provision, peace, etc. *"Whatever you ask the Father in My name He will give you"* (John 16:23).

  > **Declare:** You can declare something, and it will be established (Job 22:28, Isaiah 35:4-10). It's remarkable that often the Lord wants us to participate in and enjoy something of the creative authority that He has. A declaration is where we speak out a desired outcome, declare a specific scripture that is applicable in the context, or prophetically declare the will of the Lord in a situation. Things that need to be brought into existence or shifts that must occur (e.g. breakthrough in finances and debt, shifts in relationships, protection, etc.) are appropriate areas for declaration. The Lord delights to underwrite a declaration issued in faith.

  > **Command:** You can also engage directly against

the "target" (not the person!) using one or more of the "weapons" that the Lord has placed at our disposal (2 Corinthians 10:3-4). This is appropriate when dealing with demonic activity, physical afflictions, depression, storms, etc. For example, you can command an affliction to leave in the name of Jesus. (In such a situation, It's helpful to be as precise as possible. If you know the specific medical condition, name it.) Scripture mentions several weapons, including:

- Word of God (Ephesians 6:17, Hebrews 4:12)

- Name of Jesus (Philippians 2:10)

- The Blood of the Lamb (Revelation 12:11)

- The Word of Your Testimony (Revelation 12:11)

- The Word of Prophecy (1 Timothy 1:18)

- The Weapon of Righteousness (2 Corinthians 6:7)

• Don't worry if at first you are not sure which type of prayer to use. It's more important that you engage, and adjust as you go (see Review later). With experience and growing sensitivity to the Holy Spirit, the right approach will become more evident.

8.4. Engage!

- This is the critical event, and we want to get to this point as quickly as possible.

- Encourage the person to just relax and receive.

- Pray for effect. Our objective is to secure breakthrough, not just to go through the motions!

- Pray short impactful prayers. As mentioned earlier, long prayers are not necessary or helpful.

- Stick with the type of prayer that seems to be working.

- Try something different if no further progress is evident.

- Consider the tone of your praying. For example, when praying for peace for the individual, praying with a calm soothing tone is appropriate. Conversely, a forceful tone is appropriate when breaking the hold of depression on a person.

- However, avoid in speech or action anything that will produce confusion, offense or harm.

8.5. Review

- In Review we assess progress, and respond accordingly.

- Ask the person what's happening – if they feel any change. Some people may feel, heat, cold, or any number of sensations. Note however, that it is not necessary that the person feel anything – for example, only about 50% of people who are healed actually feel anything at the time. It is however a useful indicator.

- Reciprocally, let them know if you sense something happening.

- If the prayer is for healing, ask the person if they can check it out (e.g. move, bend, feel a reduction in pain, etc.).

- It's useful to ask what percentage improvement they feel... is it 50% better, 80% better, 100% better?

- Reengage based on the feedback. If certain prayers seem to be working, keep on using them. Otherwise, try something different.

- Repeat the short prayers and review again until the result is achieved, the person indicates they are done, shows discomfort, becomes restless or disconnected, or you feel prompted to stop.

- Do NOT advise the person to stop medication without consulting their doctor.

- For a healing, ask them to obtain third-party

verification (e.g. from their doctor, X-Rays, etc).

• Where it is not possible to determine the impact at the time of prayer, ask the person to provide feedback as soon as they can confirm the outcome.

• When done, ask the person to complete a testimony card once they have confirmed the answered prayer.

• On occasion, it may be appropriate to arrange to follow up with the person during the week. Some situations warrant this higher level of commitment and resolve to achieve and sustain the breakthrough.

• Note: For some, it may be more of a battle to achieve the initial breakthrough, but is readily sustained thereafter. For others, the opposite is true – the challenge is to sustain the breakthrough over time. Our goal is sustained breakthrough!

9. Guidelines for Catching

• It is never our purpose that someone fall when being prayed for, but it is common that people are so overcome with the power & presence of God that they do fall. Be prepared for this.

• Be constantly aware of your surroundings and ensure there is space should the person fall. Keep your eyes open so you can see what's happening.

- Make sure you have the strength to catch the person. Change out if you have concerns, or have someone else to assist. Have the person sit for prayer if appropriate.

- Have one foot slightly ahead of the other so you are balanced.

- Periodically touch the person's shoulder or back lightly while they are receiving prayer. This indicates to them that you are still there, allowing them to relax and receive prayer.

- If the person falls, don't try take their full weight directly on yourself. Rather, step back slightly while simultaneously guiding them gently to the ground with your hands between their shoulders.

- Do NOT place your hands under their arms or on the sides of the person, particularly if a woman.

- Try maintain the person's dignity. When available, use cloths to cover a persons exposed areas such as upper legs and midriffs.

10. Frequently Asked Questions (FAQ)

10.1. When should the leaders anoint with oil (James 5:16)?

Firstly, we should note that this is an available option, not a command. We also want to maintain a focus on the fact that all believers can and should exercise the gifts of the Spirit, and it is not the exclusive domain of leadership. That said, there are occasions where it makes sense for the pastor or leader to anoint with oil. One such case is where a serious illness exists, and anointing and prayer by a leader can produce the increased focus and unity necessary for breakthrough. Another case is where a person specifically requests prayer from a leader, perhaps because they have not yet come to understand that regular members can have as much faith for healing. In this case prayer by the leader could be more fruitful. A final note: It's important to make sure that we don't turn anointing with oil into a ritual, which could leave the impression that this act has greater power than the Name of Jesus.

10.2. What if I have a prophetic word for the person?

It is not the time nor the place nor the responsibility of the Prayer Team to give rebuke, correction or direction (This is the responsibility of the pastors). If you believe you have a word that has any element of rebuke, correction or direction, bring it to one of the leaders, who will determine how to proceed.

It is entirely appropriate to provide a brief, clear word of exhortation, edification and comfort.

See "Guidelines for Giving and Receiving Personal Prophecy" booklet.

10.3. Do we respond when there is a request for groups other than the Prayer Team to minister?

No. If there was a specific call for any other group to pray (e.g. elders, deacons, group leaders), then only those groups should respond. The leader of the meeting will usually provide clear instructions, but it is entirely appropriate to approach the leader during the meeting for clarification or suggestion to involve the Prayer Team. It could be an oversight.

If you are not scheduled but the on-duty Prayer Team is being overwhelmed with more people than usual responding, please step up and assist even if you have not specifically been asked to do so.

10.4. What if there is no apparent result from the prayer?

- We all desire to see dramatic and immediate answers to prayer, but this does not always occur.

Often times the result is evidenced some time later, or perhaps not at all.

- Be careful not to assert a reason for the apparent lack of breakthrough yet - better to acknowledge our lack of understanding, and reaffirm our care, compassion and commitment to the individual.

- Encourage them that no prayer is without effect. When we pray, something ALWAYS happens.

- Do NOT allow the person to think that there is some deficiency in their faith - being willing to receive prayer is all that is required on their part.

- It is vital that the person leave the time of prayer having experienced genuine love and acceptance.

- Follow up with the person if appropriate and offer and encourage further prayer. However, be sensitive and don't force anything.

Additional Resources

Clark, Randy. *Authority to heal: Restoring the Lost Inheritance of God's Healing Power*. Place of publication not identified: Destiny Image Pub, 2016.

Hobbs, Glen, *Guide to Giving and Receiving Personal Prophecy*. Dunwoody, GA: Glen Hobbs, 2008.

Hunter, Charles, and Frances Gardner Hunter. *Handbook for Healing*. New Kensington, PA: Whitaker House, 2001.

Johnson, Bill, and Randy Clark. *The Essential Guide to Healing: Equipping All Christians to Pray for the Sick*. Grand Rapids, Mich: Chosen, 2011.

Venter, Alexander. *Doing Healing*. Cape Town, South Africa: Vineyard International Publishing, 2009.

Made in United States
North Haven, CT
11 March 2024

49832301R00015